SV

WASHOE COUNTY LIBRARY

3 1235 29012 3830

D0759184

2000

No Longer Property Of
Washoe County Library

SIERRA VIEW—CHILDREN'S

827-0169

ANIMALS

Rhinos

by Kevin J. Holmes

Consultant:
C. Dietrich Schaaf
Director of Collections
Zoo Atlanta

Bridgestone Books
an imprint of Capstone Press
Mankato, Minnesota

Bridgestone Books are published by Capstone Press
151 Good Counsel Drive, P.O. Box 669, Mankato, Minnesota 56002
http://www.capstone-press.com

Copyright © 2000 Capstone Press. All rights reserved.
No part of this book may be reproduced without written permission from the publisher.
The publisher takes no responsibility for the use of any of the materials
or methods described in this book, nor for the products thereof.
Printed in the United States of America.

Library of Congress Cataloging-in-Publication Data
Holmes, Kevin J.
     Rhinos/by Kevin J. Holmes.
     p. cm.—(Animals)
     Includes bibliographical references (p. 23) and index.
     Summary: Describes the physical characteristics, behavior, habitat, and endangered
status of the rhino.
     ISBN 0-7368-0496-X
     1. Rhinoceroses—Juvenile literature. [1. Rhinoceroses. 2. Endangered species] I. Title. II.
Animals (Mankato, Minn.)
QL737.U63 H64 2000
599.66'8—dc21   99-052544

Editorial Credits
Erika Mikkelson, editor; Timothy Halldin, cover designer; Kimberly Danger, photo
   researcher

Photo Credits
Cheryl A. Ertelt, cover
Elizabeth DeLaney, 18
Leonard Rue Enterprises, 14
Michele Burgess, 4, 6, 16
Photri-Microstock/Betty K. Bruce, 12
Robin Brandt, 8, 10
Visuals Unlimited/Ken Lucas, 20

1 2 3 4 5 6 05 04 03 02 01 00

Table of Contents

Photo Diagram 4
Fast Facts 5

Rhinos 7
Appearance 9
Homes 11
Senses 13
Behavior 15
Predators and Food 17
Mating and Young 19
Rhinos and People 21

Hands On: A Rhino's Weight 22
Words to Know 23
Read More 23
Useful Addresses 24
Internet Sites 24
Index 24

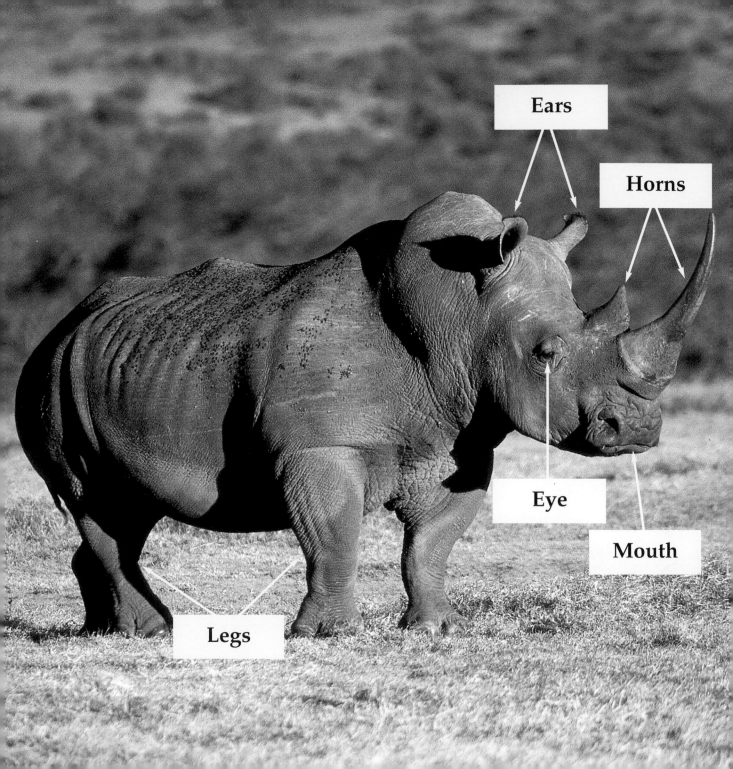

Ears

Horns

Eye

Mouth

Legs

Fast Facts

Name: Rhinoceroses are nicknamed rhinos.

Kinds: Five species of rhinos exist in the world. The white rhino, black rhino, Indian rhino, Sumatran rhino, and Javan rhino are the five kinds of rhinos. All rhino species have one or two horns on their noses.

Range: Rhinos live in Africa and Asia.

Habitat: Rhinos live on plains, in forests, or in swampy areas. Few rhinos remain in the wild. Most wild rhinos today live in national parks or on reserves.

Food: Rhinos eat leaves, grass, and other plant parts.

Mating: Male rhinos often compete with each other for the right to mate with a female. Male rhinos are called bulls. Female rhinos are called cows.

Young: A young rhino is called a calf. A calf may stay with its mother until it is 3 years old. The calf then leaves to live on its own.

Rhinos

The rhino is the second largest land mammal on Earth. Elephants are the only land mammals larger than rhinos. Mammals are warm-blooded animals with backbones. The body heat of warm-blooded animals does not change with the weather. Female mammals feed milk to their young.

Rhinos are easy animals to recognize. Rhinos have one or two horns on their noses. They have large bodies, thick legs, and very large heads. Rhinos do not have much hair on their bodies.

Five species of rhinos exist in the world. The black rhino and the white rhino live in Africa. The Indian rhino, the Sumatran rhino, and the Javan rhino live in Asia.

Scientists believe that hundreds of rhino species once lived on Earth. The most recent ancestor of the rhino was the woolly rhinoceros. This large, hairy animal lived thousands of years ago.

Rhinos have large heads and one or two horns.

Appearance

All five species of rhinos look similar. All rhinos are gray. Their bodies are round and heavy. Rhinos have short, thick legs. Their large feet each have three toes.

Rhinos have thick skin with large folds in some places. They have sensitive skin. Rhinos roll in mud to protect their skin from insect bites. The mud also keeps them cool.

All rhinos have horns. Indian rhinos and Javan rhinos have one horn on their noses. All other rhino species have two horns. Rhino horns are made of keratin. Human fingernails and toenails also are made of keratin.

Rhinos vary in size. The white rhino is the largest rhino species. The white rhino grows to be 6 feet (1.8 meters) tall at the shoulder and can weigh 8,000 pounds (3,630 kilograms). The smallest rhino species is the Sumatran rhino. This rhino is 4 feet (1.2 meters) tall and weighs 1,850 pounds (840 kilograms).

The white rhino can weigh 8,000 pounds (3,630 kilograms).

Homes

The five species of rhinos live in different areas of Africa and Asia. White rhinos live on the African plains. Black rhinos thrive in forests and in dry scrublands. Scrublands have low bushes and trees. Sumatran and Javan rhinos make their homes in the forests of Asia. Indian rhinos live in swampy areas.

Rhinos often live on territories. They mark these areas of land with their scent. Rhinos live alone or in groups on their territories. Female black rhinos may share their territory with other female rhinos. Male black rhinos live alone and protect their territory. White rhinos and Indian rhinos may live in groups. Each group usually has one adult male and several females.

Today, many rhinos live in national parks or on reserves throughout Africa and Asia. Rhinos are protected in these places. Rhinos find plenty of food and water in the parks and reserves.

Rhinos live among many animals in reserves and parks.

Senses

Rhinos have terrible eyesight. Their eyes are on the sides of their heads. Rhinos have trouble seeing in front of them. They turn their heads from side to side to look out of one eye at a time.

Rhinos depend on their senses of hearing and smell. Rhinos can hear well. Their ears can move in different directions. The rhino's sense of smell helps it avoid predators. A rhino will run away if a lion or a hyena gets too close. Few animals can move near the rhino without the rhino noticing them.

Rhinos use sounds to communicate with each other. They may grunt or scream during a fight. Mothers and calves may call softly to each other. Scientists discovered that rhinos use very low sounds that humans cannot hear. These sounds travel long distances. Rhinos can communicate with each other when they are far apart.

Rhinos smell the air to find a mate.

Behavior

Each kind of rhino has different traits. White rhinos are social. Sumatran and Javan rhinos live secretly in the thick forests of Asia. Humans rarely see them. Black rhinos are nervous when they cannot tell what is nearby. They sometimes charge to defend themselves.

Rhinos are strong and fast. Rhinos need to be muscular to carry all of their weight around. A rhino's strong muscles give it the ability to move quickly. A rhino can run as fast as 25 miles per hour (40 kilometers per hour). Rhinos can change direction quickly.

All rhinos defend themselves against predators. Rhinos sometimes must defend themselves against other rhinos who invade their territory. Rhinos charge at their opponents during a fight. They put their heads down and use their horns as a weapon. Indian rhinos sometimes use their lower teeth in a fight.

Rhinos stomp the ground and use their horns in a fight.

Predators and Food

Rhinos have few natural predators. Adult rhinos are so big and strong that few animals ever attack them. Even young rhinos are fairly safe in the wild. Female rhinos are aggressive when they defend their young. Lions and tigers are no match for a female rhino that is protecting her young.

All rhinos are herbivores. They eat plants, grasses, and fruits. They do not prey on other animals. The food a rhino eats depends on where it lives and the kind of mouth it has. White rhinos eat mainly short grass. Their wide, flat mouths are perfect for eating short grass.

Black rhinos eat leafy plants. They also eat shrubs, leaves, and tree branches. Black rhinos have pointed lips. They use their lips to pull leaves and branches into their mouths.

Sumatran rhinos and Javan rhinos eat mostly leaves, fruit, and bark. They find their food in the rain forests of Asia.

Black rhinos eat leafy plants that grow on the African plains.

Mating and Young

Most female rhinos are ready to mate when they are 5 to 8 years old. A female looks for a male rhino. She walks through other rhinos' territories. The males pick up her scent. This scent tells the males that she is ready to mate. Male and female rhinos mate to produce young.

Two males often will compete for the right to mate with a female. The rhinos use their horns to fight. After the battle, the winning male mates with the female.

A female rhino gives birth to a calf every two to three years. A calf is born 14 to 18 months after mating. Rhino calves can walk and run shortly after birth. They begin eating grass a few weeks later. But they continue to drink their mothers' milk for almost one year. Many calves stay with their mothers for up to three years. They then leave to find their own territory.

Female Javan rhinos first mate when they are 3 or 4 years old.

Rhinos and People

Few rhinos remain in the wild. They are in danger of becoming extinct. Hunters kill rhinos and sell their horns for money. People use the rhino horns for medicine and artwork.

The destruction of their habitat also is a threat to rhinos. People build and farm on rhinos' land. Rhinos will die without space to live in the wild.

People are working to protect the rhino. In some areas, killing rhinos is illegal. Some African and Asian countries have moved rhinos to national parks or reserves. These places are safe for rhinos.

Rhinos still are in danger despite the efforts to save them. Few rhinos are born in zoos. About 80 Javan rhinos exist in the world today. Nearly 9,000 white rhinos live in Africa. Fewer than 400 Sumatran rhinos live in the wild. About 2,500 black rhinos live in Africa. Only 2,000 Indian rhinos survive in the wild.

Few Sumatran rhinos still live in the wild.

Hands On: A Rhino's Weight

Rhinos are very large animals. Of all the land mammals, only the elephant is bigger than the rhino. You can learn how your weight compares to a rhino's weight.

What You Need

Scale
Piece of paper
Pencil

What You Do

1. Weigh yourself on a scale. Write down your weight.
2. Double your weight. For example, if you weigh 100 pounds (45 kilograms), add 100 plus 100. Then add 100 to that number. Add 100 again. Keep adding your weight until you reach 8,000. A white rhino can weigh 8,000 pounds (3,630 kilograms).
3. How many times did you have to add your weight to reach 8,000? How many of you does it take to equal the weight of one rhino?

Words to Know

ancestor (AN-sess-tur)—a member of a family or species who lived a long time ago; the woolly rhinoceros is the rhino's ancestor.

extinct (ek-STINGKT)—when there are no living animals or plants of a certain type living anywhere on Earth

keratin (KAYR-uh-tin)—the substance that makes up a rhino's horn; human fingernails also are made of keratin.

mammal (MAM-uhl)—a warm-blooded animal that has a backbone and feeds milk to its young

mate (MATE)—to join together to produce young

predator (PRED-uh-tur)—an animal that hunts and eats other animals

prey (PRAY) —to hunt and eat another animal

territory (TER-uh-tor-ee)—the area of land where an animal lives

trait (TRATE)—a quality that makes one thing different from another

Read More

Arnold, Caroline. *Rhino*. New York: Morrow Junior Books, 1995.

Walker, Sally M. *Rhinos*. Minneapolis: Carolrhoda Books, 1996.

Useful Addresses

International Rhino Foundation
c/o The Wilds
1400 International Road
Cumberland, OH 43732

World Wildlife Federation, Canada
245 Eglinton Avenue East,
Suite 410
Toronto, ON M4P 3J1
Canada

Internet Sites

SOS Rhino
http://www.sosrhino.org

World Wildlife Fund—Endangered Species
http://www.wwf.org/species/species.cfm?sectionid=101&
newspaperid=21

Index

Africa, 11, 21
Asia, 11, 15, 17
black rhino, 7, 11, 15, 17, 21
calf, 13, 19
herbivores, 17
horn, 7, 9, 15, 19, 21
Indian rhino, 7, 11, 15, 21
Javan rhino, 7, 11, 15, 17, 21

keratin, 9
national parks, 11, 21
predators, 15, 17
reserves, 11, 21
Sumatran rhino, 7, 9, 11, 15, 17, 21
territory, 11, 15, 19
white rhino, 7, 9, 11, 15, 17, 21